MW00532946

StudySpace

User Guide

Macintosh® and Windows®

Contents

Getting Started

Minimum System Requirements

<u>Windows:</u>

Windows® 95 and later, including Windows XP

64 MB of available RAM (128 MB RAM recommended)

10 MB of free hard disk space

Pentium II Processor, 120 MhZ or better

Monitor at 800x600 resolution or higher, with thousands of colors

Browser Netscape 4.7 and IE 4.0 and later

QuickTime® 5.0 (included)

<u>Macintosh:</u>

Macintosh® OS 8.6 and later (OSX in Classic Mode only)

128 MB of available RAM

10 MB of free hard disk space

PowerMac or PowerPC

4x CD-ROM drive

Monitor at 800x600 resolution or higher, with thousands of colors

Browser Netscape 4.7 and IE 4.0 and later

QuickTime 5.0 (included)

Installing StudySpace

<u>Windows:</u>
1.   Place the CD-ROM into the CD-ROM drive.
2.   Click on the Start button on your task bar and choose Run.
3.   Type "D:\" - where "D" is the letter of your CD-ROM drive.
4.   Double-click on Setup.exe.
5.   Follow the on-screen instructions.

<u>Macintosh:</u>
1.   Place the CD-ROM into the CD-ROM drive.
2.   Double-click on the CD-ROM icon that appears on your desktop.
3.   Double-click on the Installer file.
4.   Follow the on-screen instructions.

Once you have StudySpace installed on your computer, continue on to the section that says Setting up and Signing In.

Setting Up and Signing In

To access the program, you must first register as a user. Follow these steps to register with StudySpace:

1. Insert your StudySpace CD-ROM into your CD-ROM drive.
2. Double-click on the StudySpace icon installed on your computer. A dialogue box appears.
3. If it is your first time opening the program, click on New Student (Windows) or Add (Mac) to create a new student login and password.
4. Enter your first name or a nickname.
5. Enter a password.
6. Reenter the password to confirm. A dialogue box appears showing your name on the list of registered students.
7. Click on your name to highlight it.
8. Enter your password.
9. Click on Login.

Starting StudySpace

1. Once you have selected a name and password, click on File, then Open to locate the StudySpace file.

2. Click on the ".hmb" filename to open. The title page of your textbook appears.

3. Click anywhere on the title page. The Table of Contents will appear on your screen.

4. To continue, click on any of the chapters to begin the program. For assistance with the program, click on Tutorial which will help teach you about the different functions within StudySpace.

Getting Around in StudySpace

Knowing how to move around in StudySpace can make your learning a lot easier. There are different ways to navigate through the program and to access reference information in StudySpace. There are the **Onscreen Navigation Tools**, the **Menu**, and the **Standard Toolbar**. On the following pages, you will learn to locate and use these simple tools.

On Screen Navigation Tools

Onscreen navigation tools allow you to access individual chapters quickly by clicking on your computer screen.

Main Menu

Whether you are reading the Introduction for the first time or are already immersed in a chapter, you are only one click away from the Main Menu. From the Main Menu, you can go immediately to any chapter you want by clicking on the chapter number or title. Or while in a chapter, click on Main Menu button at the top right corner of your screen.

Chapter Table of Contents

To access individual chapter menus (like the one below), click on the chapter you want to access from the Main Menu. From within the chapter TOC, click on the page you wish to access. You may return to the chapter menu by clicking the title bar on the left hand side of the screen.

Click here to go
to video section

Click here to return to the
chapter's Table of Contents

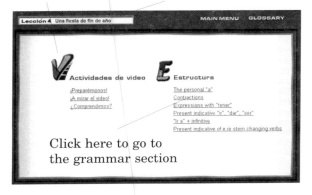

Click here to go to
the grammar section

Navigation Buttons

You can move forward and back within the program by clicking on the buttons **Back**, **Next** and **Continue** at the bottom of the page.

Grammar References

Your CD-ROM contains materials to help you with unfamiliar vocabulary and to offer useful information. References are indicated either by a label, a button or a hyperlink, as shown below.

Grammar Reference

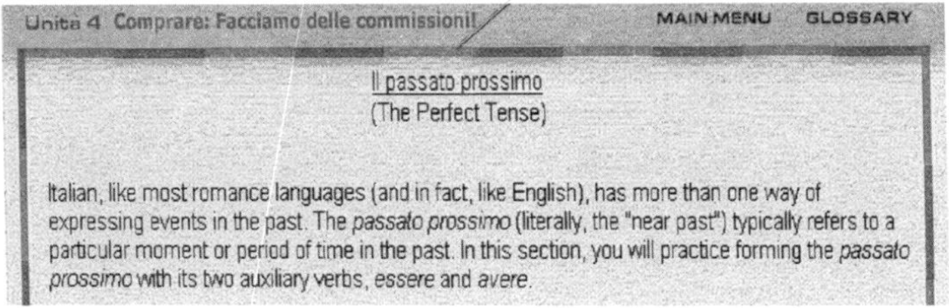

Unita 4 Comprare: Facciamo delle commissioni! MAIN MENU GLOSSARY

Il passato prossimo
(The Perfect Tense)

Italian, like most romance languages (and in fact, like English), has more than one way of expressing events in the past. The *passato prossimo* (literally, the "near past") typically refers to a particular moment or period of time in the past. In this section, you will practice forming the *passato prossimo* with its two auxiliary verbs, *essere* and *avere*.

The Menu

At the top of your screen, a menu bar displays items typically shown in software programs (for example, **File**, **Edit**, **View**, and **Help**). Three of the items on the menu, however, have been specifically designed to help you move around in StudySpace. Most of the items on the menu display keystroke shortcuts for the features described.

Textbook

The Textbook menu duplicates the function of the Back and Next buttons. It also allows you to return to the title page of your textbook.

To move around in StudySpace using the Textbook menu:
1. Click on Textbook from the menu.
2. Click on Previous Page to return to the page immediately preceding the one displayed.
3. Click on Next Page to open the next page in your CD-ROM.
4. Click on Start of Book to open the title page.

You can also access previous and successive pages by hitting the left and right hand black arrows on the tool bar or the Page Up and Page Down keys on the upper right of your keyboard. The Start of Book/Home key takes you to the title page.

Bookmarks
Bookmarks are pages you tag for your own quick access.
These may be an exercise page, a video clip that you
want to play again, or even a page in the tutorial. Before
you can jump to a bookmark, you must tag it by adding it
to your list of bookmarked pages. The process is similar
to adding a bookmark or a favorites page in your Web
browser.

To add a bookmark:
1. Go to the page you wish to bookmark.
2. Click on Bookmarks to display the Bookmarks menu.
3. Click on Add Bookmark. The page you are currently
displaying appears in the Add Bookmark dialogue box.
4. Click on OK to confirm your choice.

10

Once you have added a page to your list of bookmarks, you can go to it quickly from anywhere in the program.

To jump to another page using the Bookmark feature:
1. Select Bookmarks from the menu.
2. Select Open Bookmark. A list of boookmarks you have created is displayed.
3. Select the page you want to open.
4. Click open to go to the selected page.

History

As in a Web browser, the History function allows you to go to one of the ten most recent pages you have visited. This is very useful when you have selected a link from a particular page that takes you to another page. If you want to get back to the previous page, select **History**, select the page, and click open. The pages are listed by their names.

Other Windows Menu Bar Destinations

The menu also allows you to access StudySpace features such as the **Glossary**, the **Reference**, and the **Subject Index**. The menu also provides a way to start your word processor, your Web browser, and e-mail program while working in StudySpace.

Select the Resources menu to activate these additional tools.

Questions, Answers and Feedback

There are many different question types included in StudySpace to enhance your learning of the subject matter. In addition to the common types of questions like True/False, Multiple Choice, and Fill-in the Blank, your StudySpace CD-ROM may also use special types of questions like drag and drop, listen and record, and responses you can e-mail to your teacher. In the next few pages, you will be instructed on how to work with the various question types presented in StudySpace.

Sentence Completion I — Fill-in-the-Blank

To complete a fill-in-the-blank exercise:

1. Click on the blank to display the cursor, and begin typing.

2. Enter the word or phrase that best completes the sentence.

Click on blank to enter your answer.

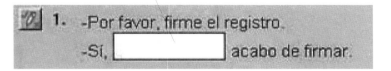

3. Click on Check Answer to evaluate your response. The Check Answer button displays a checkmark if your answer is correct, an x if not.

4. Click on Show Answer to display the correct response.

If you see feedback in a popup box, double-click on the box to make it disappear.

Audio Questions

The best way for you to be exposed to a language is to be around people or in a country where that language is spoken. If that isn't possible, you can use audio and video. Your StudySpace CD-ROM may provide you with the opportunity to listen to audio and video as well as to record your own voice so that you may compare your answer to that of the pre-recorded speaker.

To listen to an audio recording, use the following dials:

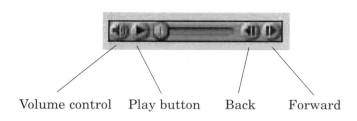

Volume control   Play button   Back   Forward

Listen and Record

To use the play and record feature, do the following:

1. Press the gray Play button to hear the question or statement.

2. Press the red Record button.

3. Speak clearly to record your answer.

4. Press the gray Playback button to review your recorded answer.

5. Press the "Correct Answer" play button.

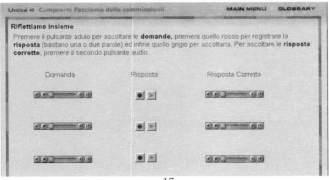

Your StudySpace CD-ROM may allow you to "take dictation" from your computer. To answer a listen-and-write question:

1. Press the gray Play button to hear the question or statement.
2. Click on the white blank space to activate the vertical cursor.
3. Enter your answer.
4. Click on the Check Answer button to confirm your answer.

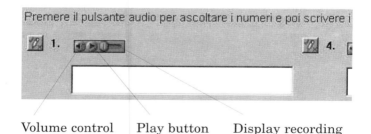

Volume control   Play button   Display recording

Drag and Drop I - Word Order

Drag-and-Drop questions can take several forms. For example, you may be asked to form a logical sentence.

To answer a Drag-and-Drop word order question:

1. Click on the box you wish to place in the sentence.

2. Holding down the mouse button, drag the box to the correct place in the row of boxes below. Make sure the border of the box turns dark before you release the mouse button.

3. On some activities, the item will return to its original place if you are incorrect. On others, you will see a Check Answer button.

Drag the words into the correct order to form a complete sentence.

| chemise | rouge | Aimes-tu | jolie | cette | ? |

Keyword Questions

Keyword questions provide you with word cues to help
you write a short "essay" answer. Whenever you use a
word from the left column correctly, it will be highlighted. In this way, you can know as you write that you are
on the right track.

To answer a keyword question:
1. Click on the blank white space to the right of the word
list.
2. Enter your answer in the white space. Left-column
words are highlighted when you use them correctly.

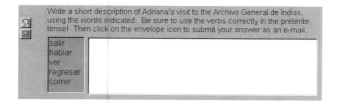

E-mailing Your Answers

On some questions, you can send your answer to your teacher by clicking on the e-mail icon under the Show Answer button. You do not have to set your email application. Your StudySpace CD-ROM will use the default e-mail application on your computer.

1. Answer the question by typing in the answer box.
2. Click on the E-mail icon to send your answer to your teacher. Your e-mail application will open with a new message.
3. Use the Paste command to copy the text of your answer into your e-mail.
4. Enter your teacher's e-mail address in the To field and send your e-mail.

Exiting StudySpace

After you have completed your work in StudySpace you are ready to exit the program. Go to File, Quit to leave StudySpace. If you would like to open the program to continue working at a later, time you must reenter your password information.

Technical Support

For technical assistance, call Houghton Mifflin Software Support at 1-800-732-3223, Monday through Friday between 9a.m. and 5p.m. E.S.T. or send an email to "support@hmco.com".